Clara Schumann

PIANO VIRTUOSO

Clara Schumann

PIANO VIRTUOSO

by Susanna Reich

CLARION BOOKS · NEW YORK

Clarion Books
a Houghton Mifflin Company imprint
215 Park Avenue South, New York, NY 10003
Copyright © 1999 by Susanna Reich
First Clarion paperback edition, 2005.

The text was set in 12.75-point Galliard.
Book design by Barbara Powderly.

www.houghtonmifflinbooks.com

Printed in the U.S.A.

Library of Congress Cataloging-in-Publication Data
Reich, Susanna.
Clara Schumann : piano virtuoso / by Susanna Reich.
p.   cm.
Summary: Describes the life of the German pianist and composer
who made her professional debut at age nine
and who devoted her life to music and to her family.
ISBN 0-395-89119-1
1. Schumann, Clara, 1819–1896—Juvenile literature.
2. Pianists—Germany—Biography—Juvenile literature.
[1. Schumann, Clara, 1819–1896. 2. Pianists. 3. Woman—Biography.]
I. Title.
ML3930.S385R45   1999
786.2′092—dc21   98-24510
[B]   CIP
AC   MN

CL ISBN-13: 978-0-395-89119-3   CL ISBN-10: 0-395-89119-1
PA ISBN-13: 978-0-618-55160-6   PA ISBN-10: 0-618-55160-3

CRW 10 9 8 7 6 5

For Nancy

CONTENTS

PREFACE *ix*

CHAPTER ONE
Frederick's Dream 1

CHAPTER TWO
The Debut 10

CHAPTER THREE
Fame—and a Special Friend 24

CHAPTER FOUR
Success and Secrets 33

CHAPTER FIVE
"Does Mr. Schumann Play, Too?" 48

CHAPTER SIX
Mother and Musician 62

CHAPTER SEVEN
The Priestess 88

EPILOGUE
Pieces of a Puzzle 101

EVENTS IN THE LIFE OF CLARA SCHUMANN *106*

INDEX *113*

PREFACE

I WROTE THIS BOOK in consultation with my mother, Nancy B. Reich. She is a musicologist, a scholar who studies the history of music. She is the author of *Clara Schumann: The Artist and the Woman* and is now working on a translation of Clara's diaries, which have never been published in English.

When my mother was first learning about Clara's life, she visited all the places Clara had lived, as well as the concert halls in which she had performed. She examined books, letters, diaries, newspapers, and music manuscripts in libraries and universities all over Europe. A single letter or newspaper review could take weeks to track down. She even looked up Clara and Robert's descendants in phone books and located and interviewed several great-great-granddaughters and other descendants. Clara's life was like a puzzle that my mother pieced together.

I was a teenager at the time my mother was doing this research, and the conversation at our dinner table was often about Clara, Frederick, Robert, Johannes, and their friends. Every day, as the pieces of the puzzle fell into place, my mother excitedly shared them with our family. She talked about Clara and Robert as if she knew them, and I regarded them as long-lost relatives.

Over the years my mother made many research trips, and after each trip I heard in great detail about all the people and places she had seen. Eventually I went with her and got to see some of these people and places for myself.

My mother's dedication to the highest ideals of scholarship has always been an inspiration. She sparked in me an enthusiasm for Clara Schumann's story. This book is the happy result.

I would like to thank the following for their assistance with illustrations: Styra Avins, Petra Diessner, Helga Heim, Gerd Nauhaus, Elizabeth Schmiedel, Herma Stamm-Bargiel, Eugen Wendler, and Maria Zduniak. Thanks are also due to Elena Ostleitner for inviting me to participate in the 1996 Vienna conference marking the centennial of Clara Schumann's death; to Julie Strauss-Gabel for her sensitive and intelligent editing; to the late Dorothy Briley for believing in my book; and to Gary and Laurel Golio for their patience, love, and understanding.

CHAPTER ONE

Frederick's Dream

ON SEPTEMBER 13, 1819, in the bustling German city of Leipzig, a baby girl was born to Marianne and Frederick Wieck (pronounced VEEK). Frederick chose the name Clara for his child, a name that means bright, or shining. In the flickering candlelight of evening, as he lifted her up from her wooden cradle and stared into her enormous blue eyes, he imagined that this tiny, squirming baby would one day grow into a great musician who would light up the world with the brilliance of her playing.

From the day of Clara's birth, Frederick dreamed of turning his little daughter into a *virtuoso*, an expert musician with dazzling technical skill. He was determined to train her to be the best pianist in all of Leipzig, perhaps in all of Germany. With his genius for teaching music, he thought, his Clara might even become one of the greatest musicians the world had ever seen.

In the nineteenth century, the people of Leipzig had neither radios nor televisions. At dusk, when families and friends gathered in their narrow wooden houses, they would entertain one another with conversation, "parlor games" like cards or charades, and music. All over the city, amateur musicians fiddled on their violins, tooted on their flutes, and skimmed their fingers over the shiny black and white keys of their pianos.

In a city with so many music lovers, an ambitious piano teacher like Frederick found no shortage of students. All day long, proper young ladies and gentlemen in starched clothes streamed in and out of the Wiecks' house, their music tucked under their arms. Downstairs, their mothers and fathers visited Frederick's piano store, where he tuned, repaired, rented, and sold pianos.

Frederick's wife, Marianne, taught piano, too. She was an accomplished singer, and had begun performing in public while still a teenager. The sound of her beautiful voice often filled the elegant Gewandhaus, the most important concert hall in Leipzig.

Marianne was a former student of Frederick's. He had always admired Marianne's musical talent, but their shared interest in music was not the only reason he had married her. He knew that Marianne's success as a singer and pianist would bring him new students and attract new customers. As his wife, the light of her talent would reflect onto him.

The market square in Leipzig, around 1830. (C. W. Arldt, Picture Collection, The Branch Libraries, The New York Public Library)

Under Frederick's watchful eye, Marianne kept a busy schedule of teaching and performing, even though she was almost constantly pregnant. In seven years she gave birth to five children. Sadly, only three survived: Clara, and her younger brothers Alvin and Gustav. Fortunately, Frederick agreed to hire nursemaids and nannies to help with the children. In the nineteenth century, even piano teachers could afford live-in servants, because servants were paid only pennies a day.

Clara and her brothers were surrounded by the force and flow of music from their earliest days. They could often feel the pounding rhythms of the piano right through the floorboards, and sometimes Marianne's lilting voice would drift up the staircase and into the nursery.

But even music could not make Frederick and Marianne's marriage a happy one. Frederick was talented and intelligent, but he could also be demanding, controlling, and stubborn. He often lost patience with Marianne and the children, and easily flew into a screaming rage. Then the sweet waves of music that enveloped the children all day long would be drowned out, and the family would be caught instead in the net of Frederick's anger.

The strain in Marianne and Frederick's marriage had a powerful and unusual effect on their only daughter: Clara did not speak a single word until she was over four years old, and then she spoke with difficulty. It seemed as if she couldn't hear or understand words. Some people even thought she was deaf or mentally retarded since she spoke so little and seemed uninterested in what was going on around her. But Frederick noticed that Clara had no trouble hearing music, and when she was five he decided she was old enough to start music lessons.

He began by teaching her little dance tunes on the piano. Clara was expected to sit silently and obediently on the bench. She would listen intently, following the movements of Frederick's arms with her big, dark blue eyes, imitating his hand positions, and trying hard to match his tones.

Frederick was a strict and demanding teacher, but Clara loved music and eagerly looked forward to her daily lessons. In spite of her father's temper, she craved his attention and desperately wanted to please him. She liked having her father all to herself, and knew that if she was cooperative he might even have a kind word for her. Besides, at the piano, no one expected her to talk. She could speak through the music without using any words.

To everyone's surprise, after Clara began music lessons her speech slowly began to improve, although it remained hesitant for years. Over time, as if by magic, her "deafness" disappeared.

It did not take Frederick long to notice that Clara's piano playing, even at the age of five, was unusually accomplished. If she heard a short piece played only once, she could repeat it without ever seeing the written music. She would sit with her back perfectly straight, her fingers searching the keys as if they had a mind of their own, and from her tiny fingertips the perfect notes of the tune would come pouring out.

Frederick realized that Clara's amazing musicianship was accompanied by a personality he could mold to his liking. She was not only talented, she was also obedient and eager to please.

His mind started to tick. He made plans. Clara could be the virtuoso he dreamed of creating. His daughter would show the world what a wonderful piano teacher he was, and bring fame and fortune to his family.

It never occurred to Frederick to ask Clara what she thought of his idea.

Unfortunately, at the same time that Clara was discovering her voice at the piano, her parents' marriage was falling apart. The little girl who

Frederick Wieck,
Clara's father.
(Archiv des
Robert-Schumann-
Hauses, Zwickau)

found it so difficult to talk watched silently as her family disintegrated. Frederick's ranting and raving, his constant demands, and his rigid attitudes forced Marianne to conclude that she could no longer live with him, even though it meant abandoning her children.

Asking for a divorce was almost impossible for a German woman of the nineteenth century. Women owned no property, and had few respectable ways to make a living. Divorce was considered scandalous and shameful; women had no rights, and laws did not protect them.

Even worse, in a divorce a mother had to give up her children. According to German law, children were the father's property. If Marianne divorced Frederick, the children would belong to him, along with the house and everything in it. Legally, Clara, Alvin, and Gustav were no different from the furniture.

Life with Frederick must have been truly unbearable for Marianne, because in 1824, when Clara was almost five, Marianne took the drastic step of moving out of the house. She and Frederick were soon divorced.

When Marianne left, Frederick was furious. He insisted, as was his right, that the children live with him. He expected his orders to be obeyed without question, and the children were allowed to visit their mother only when Frederick gave his permission.

When Clara was six, she was sent to Marianne for a visit. Frederick sent this letter along with her:

Madam! I am sending you the most precious thing in life still left to me. . . . Say nothing, if possible, about what has happened. . . . Further-

Clara's mother,
Marianne Tromlitz,
in 1816, the year
she married
Frederick Wieck.
She was nineteen
years old.
(Photo courtesy of
Herma Stamm-Bargiel)

more, give the child little pastry and make sure you do not allow any naughtiness. . . . When she practices, do not let her rush. I expect the most rigorous adherence to my wishes; if not, my anger will be incurred.

Marianne remarried, and within two years she moved to faraway Berlin with her new husband, Adolph Bargiel. After the move Clara and her brothers rarely saw their mother. Marianne and Adolph had several of their own children, and Clara's contact with her mother was limited to letters and short visits when Marianne happened to pass through the city.

Soon after her parents' divorce, Clara suffered a second blow when Frederick fired her nanny. Suddenly all of the women who had ever loved her were gone. The shy little girl with the halting speech was left with no one to comfort her, no one to talk to, no one to share her secrets or to whisper encouragement. At six, Clara was left with nothing but two baby brothers, a temperamental, demanding father, and her music.

CHAPTER TWO

The Debut

CLARA HAD LOST both mother and maidservant, but music had embraced her from birth, and in music she found some consolation for her loss. For two hours every day, the little girl whose feet still dangled from the piano bench practiced her music pieces with a concentration that was remarkable for a child her age. She began to improvise short compositions of her own, too, and when Frederick saw Clara working so diligently, he was pleased.

Gradually, through music, the tongue-tied Clara found a way to communicate all of the most important things she wished to express. In a sense, music became her first language, her "mother tongue." Through

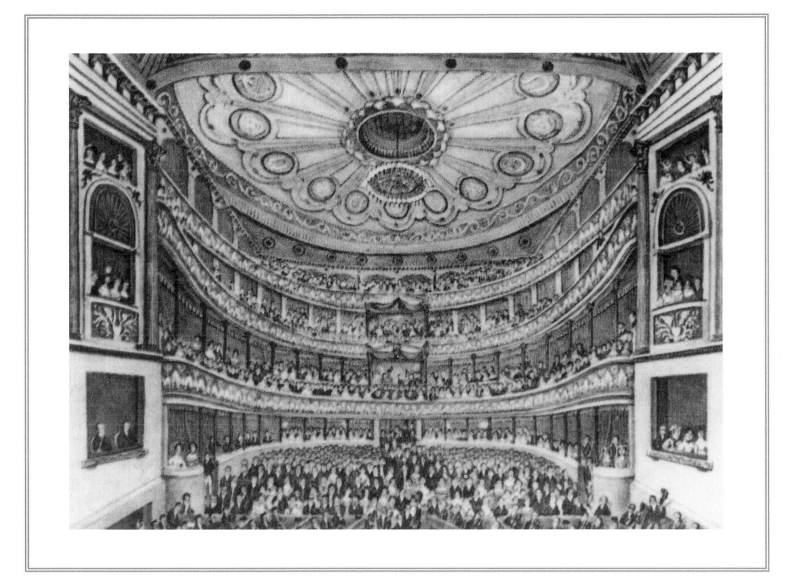

*The interior of the theater in Leipzig, where Clara was often taken
as a child to see opera and plays.*
(L. Thiele, Stadtgeschichtliches Museum, Leipzig)

music she could "speak" to her father. At her daily lessons, side by side on the piano bench with him, she found a way to share what she felt inside, without even knowing the words for her feelings.

Soon music would give her a voice in the world louder than any words she would ever speak.

Frederick took charge of Clara's training. He considered himself an expert on the subject of education because, as a young man, he had been employed as a tutor. By the time his daughter was six, Frederick was taking her regularly to the opera, concerts, and theater. At seven, she spent three hours at the piano every day: one hour for her lesson and two hours for practice. Frederick hired private tutors so that she could be taught at home rather than in school. (Private tutors were common among middle-class families during the nineteenth century.) Clara studied reading and writing, and when she was older her schedule expanded to include violin, singing, music theory, music composition, French, English, and religion.

An entry in her diary the year she was eight reads: *My father assures me that I already have a good, firm touch on the piano due in no small part to my chubby little hand, which is quite broad, as well as to the agility of my fingers (without having to use the elbows).*

Frederick commanded the household like a general, organizing not just her education, but every moment of Clara's life. Every day she was taken for a vigorous walk, which lasted several hours. She had few friends and was given no time to play with other children, except Alvin and Gustav.

Clara Wieck,
age eight.
(Archiv des
Robert-Schumann-
Hauses, Zwickau)

In 1828, Frederick remarried. Nine-year-old Clara did her best to ignore her new stepmother, Clementine. The budding musician was used to spending many hours each day with her father and hated the thought that Clementine might interfere. Frederick was as strict as a whole roomful of parents. What use was another one, especially one who couldn't even sing in tune?

Clara needn't have worried. Frederick was growing more and more enthusiastic about the musical (and money-making) potential of his talented daughter. He clung fast to his idea of creating a child prodigy whose accomplishments would show the world what a great music teacher he was.

Although Frederick acted like an ogre at times, he had a good sense of humor and many friends. He honestly thought that he was providing the very best education for Clara. He sincerely believed that his brilliantly talented daughter was happier with the rigorous schedule he provided than she would have been at school or with friends her own age.

Life in Clara's house was certainly not dull. Almost every day musicians gathered in the living room. Clara was always present as they laughed and talked, comparing notes on this composer and that, criticizing the previous night's performance at the Gewandhaus, or playing their latest compositions for each other.

One of Frederick's friends wrote about the wonderful times he had at Clara's house:

Every composer and virtuoso who came to Leipzig found that the morning or evening gatherings there offered the best opportunity to play and to hear new things. The soul of the entire proceedings was Father Wieck, who, when he was in a good mood, sparkled with humor.

As Clara's playing improved, it was for these friends of her father's that she gave her first performances. Her shyness kept her from joining in the conversation, but she sat and listened, and often played the piano for the grown-ups. They praised Clara's musicianship and marveled at her talent. Their admiration pleased her enormously, and made all her hard work worthwhile.

If Clara missed playing with other children, she never said so. Making music and spending time with adults was the only life she had ever known. It never occurred to her that life could be any different.

Before long, it became clear to Frederick's musical friends what he had long known: Clara was truly a *wunderkind,* a child prodigy. She could play difficult pieces on the piano better than most adults and was already composing. She didn't play mechanically, like a monkey that had memorized a few tricks. Clara's performances were expressive. She showed genuine feeling and musical sophistication.

In 1828, the same year that he remarried, Frederick decided Clara was ready to make her professional debut. He arranged for her to play on a program at the Gewandhaus with several other musicians. His creation was to be unveiled.

The exterior of the Gewandhaus, painted by Felix Mendelssohn in 1836.
(Whittall Collection, Library of Congress)

Clara could hardly contain her excitement. Her first public concert! The most important musicians in the world played at the Gewandhaus, and now she was to perform there, too.

The whole household was caught up in the preparations. An expensive silk dress was ordered. Clara practiced furiously. Frederick stormed about, issuing instructions to the servants, to Alvin and Gustav, and to Clementine, his new wife.

Clara's debut, on October 20, 1828, was a rousing success. The review in the weekly *Leipzig General Music Journal,* which was read all over Germany, praised both Clara and her father:

It was especially pleasing to hear the young, musically talented Clara Wiek [they misspelled her name], *just nine years old, perform . . . to universal and well-earned applause. . . . We may entertain the greatest hopes for this child, who has been trained under the direction of her experienced father, who understands the art of piano playing so well and teaches with devotion and great skill.*

The public approval was a victory for Frederick. He had earned the respect of the critics. All of Leipzig, he thought, would now recognize his superior teaching methods.

He decided to give Clara and her musical training even greater attention, devoting more and more of his time to grooming her for the concert stage. Clara didn't mind. She understood perfectly that the best way to please her father was to obey his wishes. Besides, there were other rewards. The promise of fame called for Clara to have her own room, special pianos imported from Vienna, and a closet full of elegant dresses and jewelry for performances. And she enjoyed the applause.

Meanwhile, Clementine took care of household matters and super-

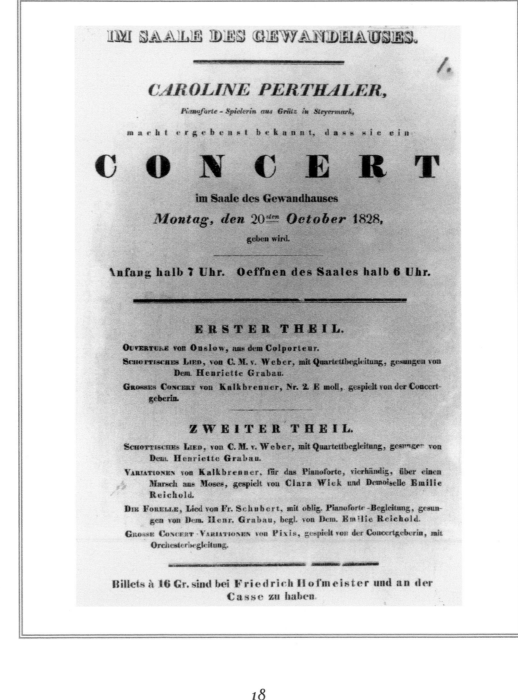

*The program
from Clara's first
appearance in the
Gewandhaus
in 1828.
(Archiv des
Robert-Schumann-
Hauses, Zwickau)*

vised Alvin, Gustav, and the servants. Even though she was Frederick's new bride, she could never rival Clara as the most important person in Frederick's life. Even when Clementine and Frederick had three children of their own, his world still revolved around Clara, and around his determination to make her a star.

As for Clara's brothers, Frederick considered them nothing but financial burdens. Alvin and Gustav were neither as gifted nor as cooperative as their sister. Unwilling to put up with Frederick's excessive demands, they bridled at his attempts to control them. Frederick had little time for them, and less patience.

Of course, even Clara occasionally misbehaved. She had spent so much time with Frederick that by now she had absorbed many kinds of lessons besides musical ones. She could be willful and stubborn, too, in her own quiet way.

If Clara disobeyed her father, she was punished. Frederick never aimed his fury at her quite as harshly as he did at Alvin and Gustav, but his words could sting. Once, when he thought Clara had played a piece poorly, he called her "lazy, careless, disorderly, stubborn, and disobedient," tore up the music, and refused to let her play her favorite pieces for several weeks. Her music was returned only after she pleaded with him and promised to be good.

Clara's piano playing was so well received in Leipzig that the ambitious Frederick soon scheduled some private concerts for her in the court city of Dresden. There, in the gilded salons of the aristocracy, she proceeded to charm everyone with her playing.

In Dresden, Clara played music by popular composers of the day as well as pieces she herself had written. The performances were a huge success. Invitations from counts and princes came pouring in. Lords and ladies flocked to hear the young girl who played so beautifully. They invited Clara to their palaces and showered her with gifts. Frederick reported it all in letters to Clementine:

> *Clara received a beautiful gold cross from a lady-in-waiting, set with lovely jewels. So far she has received sixteen presents. . . . Every day the ladies come to braid her hair. You should see how beautiful it looks. They vie with each other to pay attention to her. . . . The Princess Louise is just crazy about Clara. One Countess took the ring from her finger and put it on Clara's.*

The stories Frederick recounted in his letters revealed his pride not only in Clara's accomplishments, but in her attitude as well. Clara had confidence in her playing. She already knew how good she was. Frederick wrote:

> *I will tell you a couple of anecdotes about Clara. Yesterday a Count invited her to come and play piano duets with his wife. (His wife, the Countess, is one of the leading pianists of Dresden.)*
> *And Clara's answer was, "Oh, I will certainly come, but can your wife play like me?"*

The interior of the Gewandhaus. The rectangular shape of this historic hall,
called a "shoe box" design, was copied by architects all over the world.
(G. Theuerkauf, Stadtgeschichtliches Museum, Leipzig)

The piano Clara played at her Gewandhaus debut in 1828.
(Archiv des Robert-Schumann-Hauses, Zwickau)

"Yes indeed!" the Count answered.
So she said to him, "Then take me to her. I want to get to know her."

In another letter Frederick shows how Clara endeared herself quite naturally to her audience by acting just like the ten-year-old she was:

She played for a large group of lords and ladies on a very bad piano, but she played beautifully all the same. When she finished the whole audience applauded. She stood up and said with a serious face, "Now you are clapping, and I know very well that I played badly." And some tears rolled down her cheeks. The anecdote is now the talk of the town.

Clara and Frederick remained in Dresden for one month. In April, they returned triumphantly to Leipzig to prepare for Clara's first solo concert at the Gewandhaus, which was to take place in November. The brilliant light of Clara's promise was beginning to shine.

CHAPTER THREE

Fame—and a Special Friend

IN 1828, THE SAME YEAR that Clara made her debut at the Gewandhaus, a shy and gifted young musician became a frequent visitor at her home. His name was Robert Schumann, and he was destined to play a most important role in Clara's life.

Robert was eighteen, and though he knew he might be considered too old to begin a musical career, he possessed a passionate desire to follow his "guardian angel" to music. When he heard Clara play at the home of a mutual friend, he was impressed, and sought out her father for lessons.

Robert's mother had grave doubts about his dream. She thought it unwise for him to abandon his legal studies and, in an emotional letter,

Robert Schumann, at sixteen. Robert was interested in both literature and music. He founded a literary society with his high-school friends. (Archiv des Robert-Schumann-Hauses, Zwickau)

This portrait of Clara was drawn in Paris in 1832. "She plays with as much strength as six boys," said the famous writer Johann von Goethe of the twelve-year-old pianist. (E. C. Fechner, Archiv des Robert-Schumann-Hauses, Zwickau)

begged for Frederick's advice. Did he think it was advisable for Robert to devote himself to becoming a musician?

Frederick responded with confidence, boasting about Clara and his own prowess as a piano teacher. He admitted that Robert was undisciplined, but felt he should be given a chance. The young man's natural musical talent and creativity evidently appealed to Frederick. The stern teacher decided to accept Robert as a student, but only if he agreed to a long list of requirements: daily lessons, diligent practicing, plenty of boring piano exercises, and a more serious attitude.

Robert was not intimidated. He had tried several teachers, but none had impressed him as much as Frederick. By 1830, Robert had enthusiastically agreed to all of Frederick's conditions and had moved in with Clara's family to begin his training in earnest.

Robert settled into a routine of daily lessons and practice that was much like Clara's. It must have been discouraging for him because Clara, who was only eleven, played far better than he did. Still, he excelled at composing, and his lively imagination found a perfect outlet in writing poetic music.

For Clara, Robert's presence was a delight. He brought laughter, friendship, and excitement into her serious life. His playful, inventive nature charmed her. Years later, Clara's daughter wrote about this time in her mother's life:

Evenings were the nicest time. Robert would fetch the children—Clara and her two brothers, Alvin and Gustav—to his room, and here he

would become a child again with the children. He told them his best sto-
ries and played charades with them; he teased and frolicked and had the
little boys taking turns standing on one leg—the one who could hold out
the longest received a prize. Or he appeared clothed as a ghost, so that they
ran from him shrieking. . . . So, in this way, Robert was the biggest child
of all and brought something of the sunshine of childishness to the seri-
ous life of his little friend. One can imagine how she loved him.

Of course, Robert's presence did not keep Clara from her work. Her reputation as a wunderkind was growing, and Frederick's fame as a piano teacher was growing hand in hand with his daughter's renown.

Eventually Frederick decided his talented daughter was ready to perform in Paris, then considered by Europeans to be the music capital of the world. In 1831, twelve-year-old Clara and her father left her younger brothers and pregnant stepmother, and Frederick's pupils and piano business, and embarked on a seven-month tour that would take them from Leipzig to Paris and back.

The plan was for Clara to perform in cities all along the way, building her reputation and spreading the word about her talent far and wide, until they reached the great French city. Then, in Paris, Clara's triumphs would be crowned by international fame.

The bumpy coaches that took father and daughter from town to town were crowded, cold, and uncomfortable, but Clara did not seem to mind. Her father's letters home were full of complaints about the expensive

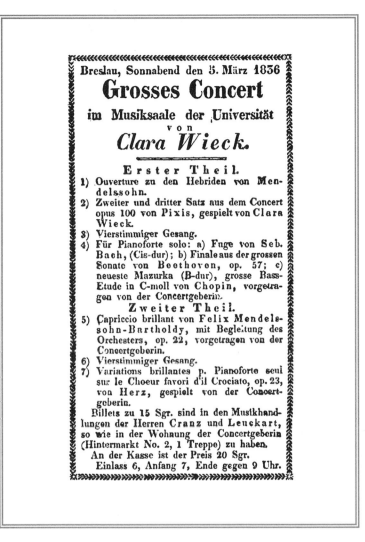

Clara's concerts were advertised in newspapers. This ad from 1836 lists the time of the performance, the price of tickets, and where tickets could be bought.
(Photo courtesy of Professor Maria Zduniak)

hotels, the high cost of food, the rude servants, and the stupid music critics who doubted his daughter's genius. But for Clara the performances were exhilarating.

Her playing received wonderful reviews in almost every town she visited. Audiences and professional musicians alike marveled not only at the beautiful sound she created at the piano, but at her musical maturity. One reviewer wrote in the *General Music Journal:*

> *Even in her first piece, the artist who is still so young received thunderous applause that grew more enthusiastic with each piece she played. And indeed, the great skill, assurance, and strength with which she plays even the most difficult movements is highly remarkable. Even more remarkable is the spirit and feeling of her performance; one could scarcely wish for more.*

Frederick played the role of concert manager, booking the halls and hotels, writing letters to important music critics, and arranging for Clara to meet influential people in each town. He selected the music she would play, decided the price and ordered the printing of the tickets, saw to it that she had appropriate dresses, and busied himself with the innumerable details of organizing a concert tour.

To Frederick also fell the important task of handling the money Clara earned at her performances, which was a significant amount. Often he would stand at the door of the concert hall, personally collecting the money as the audience poured in.

Because he had been poor as a child, Frederick placed great importance on money. He recorded all of Clara's earnings in her diary, and also noted the cost of gifts he bought her, such as jewelry. If he thought she

Clara and her father took this miniature keyboard instrument on tour with them when Clara was a child. It is called a physharmonica.
(Archiv des Robert-Schumann-Hauses, Zwickau)

had played very well, he might give her a little spending money so that she could buy herself a treat. Most of her earnings he invested in bonds. He believed he had a right to keep all the profits from Clara's concerts, since he had trained her, managed her career, and sacrificed so much of his time to do so. Legally her money belonged to him. Years later she would have to sue him for its return.

Although the performances in Paris did not bring Clara as much fame as her father had hoped, the tour was still a success. The taste of fame and money encouraged Frederick. Over the next few years he scheduled frequent concert tours, and Clara's playing continued to receive tremendous acclaim.

But troubles lay ahead for the famous wunderkind and her hardheaded father. Clara became a teenager, and Frederick discovered that seeds of rebellion were beginning to sprout in the girl who had once been so compliant. Soon he could hear the echo of his own forceful personality sounding from within his gifted daughter.

CHAPTER FOUR

Success and Secrets

I N A LETTER Frederick wrote to his wife while on tour in 1834–5, he described Clara with these words:

Clara now is often so inconsiderate, domineering, full of unreasonable opposition, careless, totally disobedient, rude, prickly, blunt, monstrously lazy . . . she gets up at nine o'clock and isn't ready until ten-thirty, then receives visitors, is invited to dinner at noon, and in the afternoon is desperately unhappy if she should have to play [the piano], because then she is thinking only of the theater and—the gentlemen. In short, what will become of her, God only knows. . . . I can't sell my pianos because she is so thoughtless that she complains about them in front of other people.

Clara in 1835.
The music is a
piano concerto that
Clara wrote when
she was thirteen.
(J. Giere, Archiv des
Robert-Schumann-
Hauses, Zwickau)

Sharp words must have been exchanged between Clara and her father during this period. Yet according to the reviews, Clara's heavenly piano playing seemed immune to the stresses of adolescence. Her musical training had been so thorough that her powerful technique carried her through, despite any emotional turmoil she may have felt. And, of course, her love of the romantic music she played must have provided an outlet for her feelings.

Her repertory included her own compositions, works by young composers like Frédéric Chopin, Felix Mendelssohn, and Franz Liszt, and music by famous masters of earlier times like Johann Sebastian Bach and Ludwig van Beethoven.

When Clara played pieces by her favorite composers, the beauty of their music could transport her through time and space. At times delicate and at other times fierce, the notes seemed to have the power to swoop down and lift her up into a world beyond words, beyond the endless demands of her father and her everyday life.

During these teenage years Clara's friendship with Robert Schumann grew closer. From the beginning it had been both a musical and a personal relationship. When Robert's first compositions were published in 1831, Clara eagerly learned them. From that time on, she often included his pieces on her programs. One of her favorites was *Papillons (Butterflies)*, in which the notes rush forward with a cascade of sound only to stop suddenly as if suspended in midair like a butterfly hovering over a flower. Robert perfectly captured the swooping, soaring movement and the exquisite colorations of the fluttering butterfly wings.

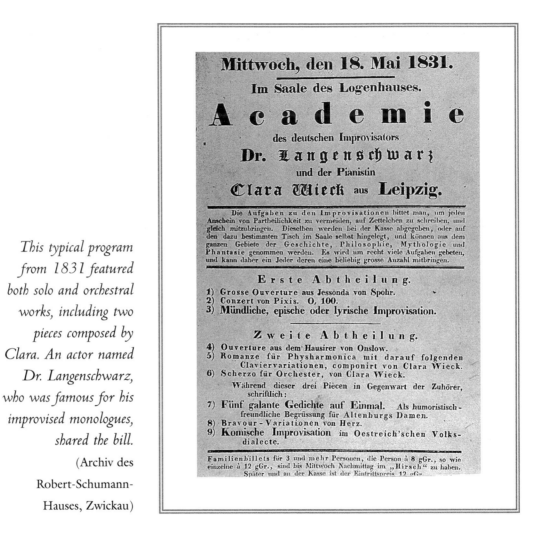

This typical program from 1831 featured both solo and orchestral works, including two pieces composed by Clara. An actor named Dr. Langenschwarz, who was famous for his improvised monologues, shared the bill.
(Archiv des Robert-Schumann-Hauses, Zwickau)

At first Clara regarded Robert as a playful friend who delighted her with his games. But by the time she was sixteen, she had fallen deeply in love with him. She realized this was a major problem. How could a busy performing career leave time for love, and what would be the reaction of her domineering father?

36

For the first time in her life, Clara decided that her father's opinion didn't matter. Still, she knew Frederick well enough to keep her feelings about Robert secret from her father for several months.

Robert was in love with Clara, but had very mixed feelings about her father. Robert described Frederick to friends as "great and noble" and an excellent teacher, but he also thought Frederick was arrogant, abusive, and insulting. He found his teacher's interest in money excessive and referred to him as *Meister Allesgeld* (Master All-for-Money). Furthermore, Robert was horrified at the way Frederick treated Alvin and Gustav. In 1831, Robert wrote in his diary:

> *Yesterday I saw a scene which I will never forget. . . . [Frederick] is surely a wicked man. Alvin had not played well: "You wretch, you wretch—is this the pleasure you give your father?" He threw him on the floor, pulled him by the hair, trembled and staggered, sat still to rest and gain strength for new feats, could barely stand on his legs anymore and had to throw his prey down. The boy begged and implored him to give him the violin, saying he wanted to play. I can barely describe it—and to all this . . . Clara smiled and calmly sat herself down at the piano with a Weber sonata. . . . Am I among humans?*

When the temperamental Frederick learned that Clara and Robert were in love, he flew into a jealous rage. While he may have admired Robert's musical talent, a personal involvement with his famous daughter was another matter entirely. Furious, he informed Clara that if she so much as saw Robert again, he would shoot him.

Frederick immediately scheduled a long concert tour to keep Clara away from Leipzig. To set matters straight with Robert, he sent the young man a letter telling him that he was no longer permitted to have any connection with Clara or the Wieck household.

For a year and a half Clara and Robert were forbidden to meet or communicate. Even if they passed each other in the street, they were not allowed to talk. However, the young lovers found a way to exchange secret letters through friends. In writing, they swore their eternal love and made plans to marry. Only once, in February 1836, did they manage to meet secretly.

In the meantime, Clara and her father departed for an extended stay in Vienna. In the ornate capital of the Austrian Empire, the eighteen-year-old Clara achieved heights of success beyond anything she and her father had ever dreamed. She became the toast of all Vienna.

Newspapers sang her praises, musicians honored her, and she was invited to dine with the highest nobility. Restaurants served a cake named after her, *torte à la Wieck,* a delicate pastry layered with whipped cream and adorned with swirls and rosettes as extravagant as the Viennese architecture. People rushed to order this "ethereal, light dessert that flew into the mouth of the eater."

She played so brilliantly for the emperor that he conferred a title on her: Royal and Imperial Chamber Virtuoso.

By 1836, Clara
was already in love
with Robert, but her
father was determined
to keep them apart.
(E. v. Leyser, Stadt-
geschichtliches Museum,
Leipzig)

Frederick was ecstatic. For a young musician to achieve such phenomenal success was unheard of. But for someone who was not only a foreigner, but also a woman, a teenager, and a Protestant in a Catholic country, it was astonishing. The Viennese audiences stormed the box office; the police had to be called in to restore order. Frederick wrote home to Clementine:

All Vienna is saying that no artist has ever made a sensation like this. . . . Now comes the reward—now the whole world shall know there is only one Clara, a Clara at whose feet all Vienna lies.

The acclaim must have come as a welcome relief to Clara, who was struggling between her forbidden love for Robert and her allegiance to her father. Her confidence was bolstered by the applause. But the success was bittersweet. Her father permitted her to perform Robert's music, which enhanced his reputation as a composer, but still forbade her to see him.

For his part, Robert was steadfast in his support of Clara's artistry:

I have heard you play only twice in two years. . . . It seemed to me, however, as though it were the most perfect playing one could imagine; I will not forget how you played my Etudes. The way you portrayed them, they were absolute masterpieces—the public cannot possibly understand how to value them—but there was one person sitting in the audience—and though his heart was pounding with other feelings, at that moment his whole being paid homage to you as an artist.

In Vienna, the constant performing and socializing was hard work, even for an energetic young woman of eighteen. She wrote to Robert:

How much one has to do in order to leave a town with a few dollars! While you are sitting at the coffeehouse at 10 o'clock in the evening, or are going home, I, poor thing, am just arriving at a party, where I have to play to people for a few pretty words and a cup of warm water and arrive home, dead tired, at 11 or 12 o'clock, gulp a mouthful of water, lie down and think, "Is an artist much more than a beggar?" And yet, art is a beautiful gift. What, indeed, is more beautiful than to clothe one's feelings in sound, what a comfort in sad times, what a pleasure, what a wonderful feeling, to provide an hour of happiness to others. And what a sublime feeling to pursue art so that one gives one's life for it.

With a constant stream of criticism, Frederick almost succeeded in driving the young lovers apart. He filled Clara's head with doubts by belittling Robert and telling her lies: that Robert would never be able to support her, that marriage would mean an end to her career. He tried every way he knew to convince Clara to forget Robert, and claimed that he would disown her and no longer be her father if she married Robert.

Clara was frightened and confused. When she shared her feelings with

Robert Schumann in 1839. He thought the portrait flattering and sent it to Clara.
She wrote: "Every time I look at it a happy shiver comes over me. I would like to sieze
it, hug it, kiss it. When I look at your mouth I hear you saying, 'My dearest Clara.'
How beautiful love is, painfully beautiful."
(J. Kriehuber, Archiv des Robert-Schumann-Hauses, Zwickau)

Robert, he became depressed. He wrote that he was haunted by nightmares and afraid that Clara would abandon him.

She wrote to him:

If anyone asks if I have already seen you, tears spring to my eyes. . . . You are so near and yet I cannot see you. . . . I am suspended in heaven and immediately afterward am so unhappy because I cannot embrace you right away, you who are everything to me, you who have opened another world to me. . . . You are the ideal of a man, an ideal I have always carried in my heart.

The secret correspondence continued, growing more passionate with each passing day. In May 1838, Clara and her father returned home from Vienna. Clara's resolve to marry Robert had strengthened in spite of her father's opposition. Angered, he announced that she could go on her next tour by herself.

Terrified that Frederick might discover the secret letters, and torn between father and lover, the young virtuoso poured her feelings into her music. In August she wrote to Robert:

How love makes one so receptive to everything beautiful. Music is now quite another thing for me than it used to be. How blissful, how full of longing it sounds; it is indescribable. I could wear myself out now at the piano, my heart is eased by the tones and what sympathy it offers! . . .

Oh, how beautiful music is; so often it is my consolation when I would like to cry. I have Father to thank for [music] *and will* never *forget this.*

The following January Clara departed for Paris without her father. To his annoyance, she gave several successful concerts there without any help from him.

According to German law of the time, children of any age were required to have their parents' consent in order to marry or else had to seek permission from the courts. In June 1839, Robert and Clara tried

Clara at twenty, the summer before she was married.
(J.H. Schramm, Archiv des Robert-Schumann-Hauses, Zwickau)

one last time to obtain Frederick's consent to marry, but he stubbornly refused. They had no choice but to appeal to the courts for permission.

Upon returning from Paris, Clara found herself locked out of her father's house. Most of her clothes and music were inside. She was not allowed in, even to retrieve them. As winter approached she sent a servant girl to fetch her coat, and her father said to the girl, "Who is this Mademoiselle Wieck?"

For several months, she was forced to stay with her mother and stepfather in Berlin. During this time, Clara was able to renew her relationship with her mother, and they remained close for many years.

Robert was so distraught over the situation that he was tortured by thoughts of death. His doubts were unbearable for Clara. In January she wrote in her diary:

My state of mind is indescribable—I cannot forget the words in Robert's last letter—they torture me. I have endured everything. I have lost my father, I have stood up to him in a court of law, what battles have I fought with myself, but Robert's love made up for all this. I believed his faith was immovable, and now he hurts me so much. I can barely calm myself.

In court, Frederick filed papers full of preposterous lies about Robert's personality and Clara's inability to run a household. Fortunately, it was easy for Robert to convince the court that none of it was true.

But the young couple had other problems. Frederick refused to give Clara any of the money she had earned in her years of performing, even though it was customary at the time for a father to provide money for his daughter's dowry. Clara resolved to earn the money herself, and undertook another tour in order to build up a bank account for her and Robert.

Meanwhile, Robert could not hide his mixed feelings about Clara's independence. The young composer was jealous of her career. He felt unsure about marrying a woman with a life outside the home, even one whose artistry he so admired.

Both of them were plagued by doubts. Right up until their marriage, each was afraid that the other might fall in love with someone else. In her diary Clara wrote:

Oh, how I tremble, how my heart pounds—I have an unhappy character. Even my great love for Robert gives me unhappy hours—I often ask myself, can I make him as happy as I would like to, as he deserves? Won't family responsibilities put too much pressure on him? Will he be recognized? Oh, my God! These and so many thoughts torture me—if I were only his wife already!

Finally, in August 1840, the court decided in Clara and Robert's favor and granted permission for them to marry. Clara returned to Leipzig from her mother's home in Berlin, and the young couple was able to make final plans for their wedding. Twenty-year-old Clara wrote in her diary:

I am trembling and quivering about the coming day with both joy and anguish. . . . I feel continuous anxiety and have never felt more exhausted. May heaven preserve my health!

She gave several more performances as Clara Wieck, and then, on September 12, 1840, she and Robert Schumann were married.

Clara and Robert were married in this Protestant church on the outskirts of Leipzig.

CHAPTER FIVE

"Does Mr. Schumann Play, Too?"

THUS BEGAN A NEW LIFE for Clara, and yet it was not so different from the one she knew. She may have been a married woman now, but she was still the famous "Royal and Imperial Virtuoso." While another female musician might have been content to retire to a life of housekeeping and child rearing, Clara Schumann had no such thought. "The practice of art is the very air I breathe," she wrote. She adored her husband, *and* planned to continue her illustrious career.

Clara's happiness was boundless, limited only by ongoing conflicts with her father. For five months after the wedding she waited for her piano to be delivered from Frederick's house, and seven months later, had to send a friend to collect the money her father had agreed to pay for

Robert and Clara, drawn while Clara toured in Vienna, 1847.
(E. Kaiser, City Archives of Bonn, Graphic Collection)

the shipping. Frederick, Clementine, and their family moved to Dresden, a German city about four hours from Leipzig by train, where he continued to teach piano and singing. Both Alvin and Gustav had left home long before—Gustav to be apprenticed to an instrument maker, and Alvin to work as a violinist. Even in Dresden, Frederick was outspoken about his contempt for Robert, publicly referring to Robert's *Spring Symphony* as the "Symphony of Contradictions." He also spread rumors that Clara and Robert had separated.

By 1842, Frederick's anger had subsided enough for him to begin making overtures of friendship to his daughter and son-in-law. Clara was moved, but Robert would have none of it. Letters were exchanged back and forth, and Clara agreed to see her father. Robert was not so easily persuaded. Insulted and resentful, he needed over a year more before he could bring himself to face his father-in-law. Finally, in 1843, the young couple finally agreed to spend Christmas with the Wiecks in Dresden. But the family relationships were forever strained.

About a year after their marriage, Clara gave birth to their first daughter, Marie. The birth of Elise followed in 1843. Perhaps Robert thought his beloved wife might now settle down into the routines of a housewife, but if he did, he was sorely mistaken. Not only was Clara independent and ambitious, she thrived on the life of a performer, savoring the applause, the attention, and the fame. Even motherhood could not compete.

Pregnancy did not prevent Clara from performing, even though at that time it was not considered polite for a pregnant woman to be seen outside the home. Clara had a career to maintain; her own mother had

Clara with her oldest child, Marie, around 1845. Photography had just been invented. (Archiv des Robert-Schumann-Hauses, Zwickau)

*Elise Schumann
at age twenty.*
(Archiv des
Robert-Schumann-
Hauses, Zwickau)

performed while pregnant. Fortunately, Clara was so popular that no one criticized her decision, and Robert's respect for her artistry was so immense that he made no effort to stop her from appearing in public. With his encouragement she also continued to compose music, writing many pieces for piano, voice and other instruments.

For Robert, marriage to the famous Clara was not easy. At first he accompanied her on many of her concert tours, but could not compose while traveling and felt snubbed when she was invited to parties without him. When she traveled to Denmark by herself in the spring of 1842, he was miserably lonely, and regretted his decision to let her go:

Still no news from you, my Clara. Have you forgotten me already? Yesterday I could hardly bear the melancholy that overwhelmed me. This desolation in the house; this emptiness in me! Letting you go was one of the most foolish things I ever did *in my life and it certainly won't happen again.*

Marie Schumann in 1869, at age twenty-eight. Clara's favorite child never married. She devoted her life to helping her mother.
(E. Bendemann, Archiv des Robert-Schumann-Hauses, Zwickau)

In 1859, Clara commissioned portraits of herself and Robert from an artist in Dresden; this portrait is based on an old photograph. It became one of Clara's favorite pictures of Robert.
(E. Bendemann, Archiv des Robert-Schumann-Hauses, Zwickau)

In 1844, Clara and Robert left their two little girls with Robert's relatives and departed on a four-month concert tour of Russia. In the capital of St. Petersburg, Clara performed for the czar and czarina. The glittering royal palace, called the Winter Palace, seemed to Clara like a "fairy tale in *The Thousand and One Nights.*"

Clara sat for her portrait, which the artist executed in charcoal. (E. Bendemann, Archiv des Robert-Schumann-Hauses, Zwickau)

In Russia audiences and critics raved about her artistry. One writer remarked:

We have had many famous pianists here, but what have we heard? Frightful noise, cannon blasts, difficult things that merely astounded; and what touched the heart? In point of fact, very little. . . . We soon forgot that they had ever visited Moscow and not one of us remembers their playing. Can we say the same of Clara Schumann? Absolutely not! The "Spring Song" of Mendelssohn, a presto by Scarlatti, fantasies by Liszt . . . fugues by Bach, masterpieces by Beethoven—these works have been so vividly impressed in our hearts and memory that henceforth they will hold us captive with their sweet shackles.

But Robert was having a miserable time in Russia. The weather was harsh, the long trip over hundreds of frozen miles by horse coach, exhausting. He was plagued by illnesses, both physical and mental. Worse yet, as the husband of a famous wife, he was in an awkward position. Clara was earning all the money and getting all the attention. The constant socializing was a great strain. Robert was often withdrawn and tongue-tied. Except for the respect and recognition he received from a few knowledgeable aristocrats, he was regarded as "Clara Schumann's husband," rather than as an important composer in his own right.

Even with his beloved Clara, Robert always had a hard time communicating. Neither of them had ever been very comfortable with spoken words, so from the beginning of their marriage they kept a joint diary. Instead of talking to each other, they shared their thoughts and feelings in writing. During the Russian tour Clara was caught up in the whirl of performances and parties and never realized just how unhappy Robert was. He returned from the trip tired and discouraged.

Later that year, looking for ways to improve Robert's health, the

Schumanns decided to move to Dresden. They both felt the climate there would be good for him, and that the presence of the royal court in Dresden would be helpful to his career.

The Schumann family stayed in Dresden for six years. Robert conducted a choral group and composed some of his most famous works of music. Both husband and wife were busy teaching. They had four more children: Julie, Emil, Ludwig, and Ferdinand. Clara continued to perform, although not as frequently as before. Once she gave a concert only a week before giving birth.

Clara supervised her growing household with the help of several servants. Her energy was prodigious. In addition to performing, composing, and teaching, she helped Robert with his choral group by assisting at rehearsals, coaching, and accompanying the group on the piano.

One of the women who sang in this chorus had this to say about Clara:

I can still remember the influence that the superlative artist Mrs. Clara Schumann exerted on us as she accompanied our singing and brought us closer to an understanding of the music through her wonderful, inspired playing. One can imagine how, under this double leadership [Robert and Clara's], all the powers we possessed would grow. . . . In each gathering, it was clearly seen that one spirit dwelled in both [of them] and this was even more evident when it was our happy task to bring a new creation of Robert Schumann to the ears of the public. With what calm, with what confidence he relied on Clara to bring us closer to an under-

standing of his ideas by stressing every important note, by intensifying the nuances. And how we saw her eyes shine with enthusiasm when the beauty of the music was appreciated! . . . It is impossible to close these memoirs . . . without casting a look once again at this rare union of gifted geniuses which in Robert and Clara Schumann had been brought together by a happy destiny.

Robert's compositions were becoming better known in Germany, but in Dresden, unfortunately, his talents went unappreciated. According to Clara, the Dresden audiences were "klutzes," and the musicians there, "a fine group—first they embrace each other as 'dear colleague' and 'darling' and then they would like to scratch each other's eyes out."

In 1850, Robert was offered a job in Düsseldorf as music director of the Municipal Orchestra and Chorus. He accepted, and the Schumanns once again moved to a new city. In Düsseldorf Clara gave birth to Eugenie, their seventh child. Clara managed the household, composed, and performed to great acclaim as Düsseldorf's greatest pianist. Students arrived from all over Germany to study with her.

Clara's contributions to the family income were substantial, which proved troubling for Robert. At times he was jealous of her success. His pride was hurt by his wife's ability to earn so much more money as a performer than he could as a composer.

But Robert had worse problems. Although he was still composing beautiful pieces, his awkwardness with people prevented him from being an effective conductor. He suffered from many physical ailments, and was

Robert and Clara
Schumann
in 1850.
(J. A. Völlner,
Heinrich-Heine-
Institut, Düsseldorf)

Düsseldorf, on the Rhine River. (J. W. Krafft, Picture Collection, The Branch Libraries, The New York Public Library)

seriously depressed. His poor health led to difficulties with the new job. Clara was forced to assist with some of his musical responsibilities.

The troubled composer became increasingly disturbed. He cruelly criticized Clara's exquisite playing, leaving her in tears. He was weak and couldn't sleep; he could barely speak, heard strange sounds, and felt pains that his doctors could not explain. Once he imagined that the spirit of a dead composer had sent him a melody.

By the winter of 1854, Robert was overcome with despair. He feared he was insane and on February 26 insisted that he be sent to a mental hospital, since he "could no longer control his mind and could not know what he might do." Clara wrote in her diary that he "was so profoundly melancholy that I cannot possibly describe it."

The next day, as Clara was speaking with a doctor, Robert slipped out of the house and made his way down to the Rhine River. There, he took off his wedding ring and flung it into the icy water. Then he jumped in.

Robert did not drown. He was rescued and brought home. Clara, distraught and six months pregnant with their eighth child, agreed to send him to an insane asylum. Several days later the children watched from an upstairs window as a horse and carriage pulled into the courtyard. Pressing their faces against the cold glass, they saw Robert being helped into the carriage, and listened to the clatter of horses' hooves on the cobblestones as their father was taken away. It was the last time they would ever see him.

CHAPTER SIX

Mother and Musician

CLARA WAS DEVASTATED, but she had a family to support, and was too proud to accept the financial help offered by friends. Soon after their eighth child, Felix, was born, she began a hectic schedule of performances. She pushed herself relentlessly, touring throughout Europe and even venturing across the English Channel. While in England, she performed twenty-six times in three months.

Her friends reported that she was pale and anxious, often bursting into tears for no apparent reason. They begged her to slow down, but she refused. She was restless, her need to perform desperate.

When Clara appeared on the stage, dressed in her dark clothes, her normally serious face was strained with sadness. But when her fingers

Clara Schumann in 1854. This picture was taken when Robert was in the hospital. (F. Hanfstaengl, Archiv des Robert-Schumann-Hauses, Zwickau)

began to dance over the keys of the piano, she was transformed. Her burning emotions poured forth into the concert halls until the seats themselves vibrated with feeling.

"It often seemed to me," she wrote, "that when I played, my over-burdened soul was relieved, as if I had truly cried myself out."

Doctors at the insane asylum advised her not to visit, fearing her presence would upset Robert. For the first few months, he didn't even ask to see her, despite the fact that he knew she was pregnant. Later he wrote, but his letters revealed a mind full of confusion.

The mental hospital in Endenich where Robert spent his last years, as it looks today. (City Archives of Bonn, Graphic Collection)

Clara sent friends and relatives to check on him. One reported that he seemed fine, another that he could only whisper. His condition worsened, but still the doctors asked her to stay away from the hospital. She dutifully obeyed.

For two and a half years, Robert lived in the mental hospital while Clara toured. Not until Robert was near death, in July 1856, did the doctors finally allow her to see him. He was weak and barely conscious, but he recognized her. For two days, she sat by his side, feeding him from a spoon.

On July 29, Clara left the hospital for an hour to meet a friend at the train station. When they returned, Robert was dead.

She wrote in her diary:

His head was beautiful in death, the forehead so transparent and gently rounded. I stood at the body of my dearly loved husband and was calm; all my feelings were of thankfulness to God that he was finally free, and as I knelt at his bed I had such a holy feeling. It was as if his magnificent spirit hovered above me, oh——if he had only taken me with him!

Robert's death left Clara a thirty-six-year-old widow with seven children. (Emil, a sickly baby, had died while she was pregnant with Ludwig.) She knew that no one else was going to pay the bills; she would have to support the family all by herself. Fortunately this was a task for which she was uniquely prepared. The brilliant virtuoso called upon all

The gravestone at Robert's grave was commissioned by Clara and erected in 1880. She was buried there in 1896. (Photo courtesy of Nancy B. Reich)

her reserves of strength and perseverance. She buried her grief, and began to perform again within three months.

Now that she was a single mother, life was filled with responsibilities. Clara had always wanted to provide her children with a more normal childhood than her father had given her, but the size of her family, Robert's illness and early death, and the demands of her career made it impossible.

By the end of 1856, all but the two youngest children were in boarding school or being raised by relatives. Marie and Elise, ages fifteen and thirteen, were away at school in Leipzig. Julie was in Berlin with her grandmother, and Ludwig and Ferdinand, after a short stay with Clara's father, were sent to school in Bonn. Only Eugenie and Felix, ages five and three, remained at home with a housekeeper.

The children's situation was actually not all that unusual. During the

Clara collected flowers and leaves and pressed them in a special "flower diary." These leaves are from Robert's grave. (Archiv des Robert-Schumann-Hauses, Zwickau)

Six of Clara and Robert's eight children, in 1855.
From left to right: Ludwig, Marie, Felix, Elise, Ferdinand, and Eugenie.
Missing are Emil, who died in infancy, and Julie.
(Archiv des Robert-Schumann-Hauses, Zwickau)

nineteenth century, middle- and upper-class European children were commonly raised by servants and sent to boarding schools when they were quite young. But Ferdinand Schumann was only seven.

To Clara, motherhood was a responsibility to be shouldered with discipline and dignity. She took her job as a mother very seriously. "You wouldn't believe how difficult it is to bring up so many children so that

Robert Schumann. "Whatever your father did, saw, read, would at once shape itself into music," Clara told her children. "When he read poetry . . . it turned into songs. When he saw you children at play, little pieces of music grew out of your games." (W. Fassbender, City Archives of Bonn, Graphic Collection)

each one is educated to be a capable human being," she wrote to a friend in 1860.

Clara actually spent very little time with her children. She often missed birthday celebrations, confirmations, and holidays. When they were sick and even when they were dying, she was not always able to be with them. Still, they were very proud of her.

"The thought that Mamma had to earn every penny I needed with the 'work of her hands' often troubled me when I was a mere child, and I hated

Clara in 1857, one year after Robert's death.
(F. Hanfstaengl, Archiv des Robert-Schumann Hauses, Zwickau)

Eugenie Schumann in 1871. Eugenie wrote that her father's death cast deep shadows on her life. (Archiv des Robert-Schumann-Hauses, Zwickau)

to have to ask for new clothes," wrote her youngest daughter, Eugenie.

The Schumann children recognized that their mother was torn between her music and her family. They even talked about it with each other. Eugenie wrote:

We knew that in our mother woman and artist were indissolubly one, so that we could not say this belongs to one part of her and that to another. We would sometimes wonder whether our mother would miss us or music most if one of the two were taken from her, and we could never decide.

The children missed their mother terribly, but were comforted by the thought that their welfare was always on her mind. "But one thing I know for certain," Eugenie wrote, "that wherever she might be, we were ever conscious of her loving care, her protecting hold over us . . . she was the greatest thing we possessed in the world."

Tragically, four of the Schumanns' eight children died before their mother: Emil as a baby, Julie and Felix from tuberculosis in their twenties, and Ferdinand from the effects of morphine addiction in his early forties. Ferdinand's addiction had developed while he was being treated for rheumatism brought on by wartime military service; his death left Clara with the additional task of supporting his widow and six children.

Julie Schumann at nineteen. Julie married an Italian count. (E. Bendemann, Archiv des Robert-Schumann-Hauses, Zwickau)

Ferdinand Schumann in military uniform, age twenty. Ferdinand served in the Franco-Prussian War of 1870. (Archiv des Robert-Schumann-Hauses, Zwickau)

Ludwig, who outlived his mother by three years, suffered from severe mental illness. He entered an insane asylum at twenty-two, and spent the rest of his life there.

Clara was forced to tour ten months a year. In spite of her fame and the high fees she was paid for each concert, it cost a great deal to support such a large family. Bills for Ludwig's mental hospital, Felix's illness, and Ferdinand's treatment for drug addiction were enormous. Between concerts she would try to find time to spend a few days with some of the chil-

Ludwig Schumann,
in 1866.
(Archiv des Robert-
Schumann-
Hauses, Zwickau)

dren. Even in the summer, when she was not on tour, she practiced, taught, and wrote letters, spending several hours each day at her desk.

But the stresses of her family life never prevented her from performing and did not even seem to affect her playing. She was uplifted by her success. In 1879, with Felix near death, she confided in a letter to a friend:

Things are going very badly with us; Felix is visibly weaker every day though he still has not taken to his bed. The poor man suffers indescribably and we suffer with him. . . . I see him only for a few minutes at a time because it excites him too much, but my heart bleeds when I see him and no matter what I am doing, whatever it is, the poor sufferer is always before my eyes so that I must summon up all my strength to keep from being overcome by the pain. . . .

It was extraordinary to me that I was able to play with such freedom and strength at the concerts I gave while I was so unhappy that I could not forget my sorrow for one moment.

Clara's house in Baden-Baden, where she and the children spent ten summers. "The mornings were entirely devoted to work," wrote Eugenie. "From our earliest childhood we had all been trained in music, and practiced in turn by the clock. . . . In the afternoons we did needlework, and . . . went for long walks. . . . Our walks usually included a meal at an inn . . . and Mamma's favorite dish, pancakes with a lot of sugar, and lettuces with a lot of vinegar, was ours too." (Archiv des Robert-Schumann-Hauses, Zwickau)

Felix, the Schumann's youngest child, in 1872. "I don't know how I should contain myself with happiness if I had a son like Felix," wrote Johannes Brahms. (Archiv des Robert-Schumann-Hauses, Zwickau)

A diary entry written during the same period tells more:

On the 14th I played in the Museum concert, an engagement promised some time ago. It was frightfully difficult, alas, and I wished I had not done it. Had I known how near the end was for our sufferer I would not have done it. My heart bled as I said good night to Felix and went to the concert. The contrast was so dreadful. Throughout the entire concert I saw only him, his emaciated body, his lifeless appearance, and alas, his lack of breath——it was horrible. And yet I played quite well, without even one wrong note!

Felix died two days later. He was twenty-four.

So many sorrows might have overwhelmed a woman with a weaker spirit, but Clara had enormous physical and emotional strength. She immersed herself in her work and found in music the comfort she needed. Years later, when Ferdinand died, Clara returned to teaching the day after the funeral.

"Work is always the best diversion from pain," she wrote.

Clara believed that her strict upbringing was the source of her strength. In a letter of 1882 she said that she had never missed playing with dolls and praised her father's "genius as an educator. . . . To my sorrow I must say he was never given the recognition he deserves. . . . I have thanked him all my life for his so-called cruelties."

When Frederick died in 1873, she wrote in her diary:

I had loved him dearly and often I had been conscious of it, but now my emotion quite overpowered me. If only I could have had one more look from him. Although we had many disagreements it never affected my love for him, a love which all my life long has been heightened by gratitude. How many years he dedicated to me, to the exclusion of all else. What a wonderful influence he had over me in helping me understand the

*Frederick Wieck
in 1853.*
(Archiv des
Robert-Schumann-
Hauses, Zwickau)

beauty of a practical, active life. How many wise rules of conduct he gave me, and not only that, but he took care that I followed them. . . . And so a man of rare character passed away—I cannot express the depths of my grief—he had been everything to me in my childhood, and now death had ended it.

Through the years of personal turmoil, Clara's many friendships also helped to sustain her. When Robert was first hospitalized, a group of close friends stood by Clara's side. Many were musicians. One was a young composer and pianist, whom both Clara and Robert liked very much. One morning in 1853, he had arrived on their doorstep, a handsome young man with long blond hair and a backpack full of his own music compositions.

Marie wrote years later:

He had barely played a few measures when my father interrupted and ran out saying, "Please wait a moment, I must call my wife." The midday meal that followed was unforgettable. Both parents were in the most joyful excitement—again and again they began and could not speak of anything but the gifted young morning visitor, whose name was Johannes Brahms.

The Schumanns recognized Johannes's rare musical talent and encouraged his composing. Robert referred to him as a "young eagle . . .

Johannes Brahms in 1853, the year he first met the Schumanns.
Robert described the young composer as "springing forth,
fully armed, like Athena from the head of Zeus; a young man over
whose cradle graces and heroes have stood watch."
(J. J. B. Laurens, City Archives of Bonn, Graphic Collection)

Clara's friend Emilie List, at age twenty-three. Clara and Emilie met in their early teens and became very close, although Emilie was not a musician. (Self-portrait, reprinted with permission from *Das Band der ewigen Liebe: Clara Schumanns Briefwechsel mit Emilie und Elise List,* Eugen Wendler, editor)

a mighty Niagara . . . the true Apostle." Johannes, in turn, called Robert "the Master."

During Robert's hospitalization, Johannes devoted himself to helping the Schumann family. He rented a room nearby and spent most of his time at Clara's house, keeping track of household expenses, arranging the books and music, and helping with the children. In doing so he earned Clara's lifelong gratitude. Clara, in return, used her influence to promote the young man's exquisite music. In time he came to be recognized, along with Robert Schumann, as one of the greatest composers of the nineteenth century.

Clara and Johannes regarded each other as best friends. It was a friendship infused with love and mutual respect. As time went on and Johannes's career took him away from the Schumann household, they kept in touch by letter. Eventually they lived in different cities but saw each other as often as possible.

Diaries and letters reveal the nature of their friendship. At first, Johannes was in awe of the famous pianist, who was almost fourteen years older than he, but gradually their shared passion for music brought them closer. They constantly advised each other on musical matters. Johannes asked for Clara's opinions on his new compositions, sending her manuscripts as soon as they were finished, asking for her suggestions and comments. Her responses were almost always enthusiastic.

"It was a pure delight—something one is rarely given," she wrote after playing his third violin sonata for the first time. "In the surging of harmonies in the first movement, I always have the feeling that I am soaring in the clouds. I love this sonata indescribably—each movement of it!"

Clara wanted to know what Johannes thought of her playing. She valued his advice on job offers, publication of Robert's pieces, and child rearing, and rarely made an important decision without discussing it with Johannes in letters.

Beside Johannes, Clara had many other friends, both men and women. Among them were some of the most famous musicians of the

Johannes Brahms in the 1860s. "He cared nothing for polite manners, but as he was at times painfully conscious of his awkwardness, he was rather shy as a young man and tried to hide this shyness under a certain bluntness," wrote Eugenie. "We knew that he was devoted to [our mother] with his whole soul. . . . In spite of his brusque ways he loved and admired her more than anyone else in the world." (C. Jagemann, Historisches Museum der Stadt Wien)

day. Because Clara traveled so much, she sustained these friendships by mail. She also carried on a correspondence with musical colleagues, publishers, and, of course, with each of her children. Once, her son Felix complained that the letter writing took too much of her time. She replied:

> *You have to consider how many people I get to know on my tours and how fond I become of them, how they always shower me with love and kindness, and all I can give them in return is constancy. . . . I do not like to offend people who have been close to me; there are so many now that even if I keep in contact with just some of them, my correspondence is still very large. Above all, however, it is naturally my deepest desire to communicate as regularly as possible with all of you* [children]—*those dearest in the world to me.*

By nurturing her friendships and her network of musical colleagues, and above all by devoting herself heart and soul to her music, Clara was able to maintain a luminous career in spite of the difficulties of raising seven children. Although at times motherhood was clearly more a burden to her than a source of joy, Clara loved her children. As both mother and financial provider for her large family, her love was expressed through devotion to her musical career. That career, which took her away from them time and time again, not only enabled her to support her family financially, but gave her the strength to persevere in the face of profound

The singer, actress, and composer Pauline Garcia-Viardot, a close friend of Clara's.
Viardot built a little theater in the garden of her villa in Baden-Baden.
An invitation to one of her performances there was considered a great honor.
The King and Queen of Prussia were among the frequent guests.
(Music Division, The New York Public Library, Astor, Lenox and Tilden Foundations)

Clara often performed with her friend, the violinist Joseph Joachim (shown here in Berlin in 1854). Since there was no electricity, they played by candlelight.
(A. v. Menzel, Archiv des Robert-Schumann-Hauses, Zwickau)

86

personal tragedy. In 1854, as she was preparing to leave the children for a tour only months after Robert's suicide attempt, she wrote in a letter to a friend, the violinist Joseph Joachim:

> *I always pray to God to give me the strength to successfully overcome the frightful agitations that I have lived through and that still await me. My true old friend, my piano, must help me with this! . . . I always believed I knew what a splendid thing it is to be an artist, but only now, for the first time, do I really understand how all my pain and joy can be relieved only by divine music.*

CHAPTER SEVEN

The Priestess

FOR THIRTY-FIVE YEARS after Robert Schumann's death, Clara performed triumphantly in Germany, Russia, Denmark, Austria, Holland, Belgium, Hungary, Switzerland, and England. In fact, her performing career lasted longer than that of almost any other musician of the nineteenth century. Concert programs exist for 1,299 performances of Clara's, and that number does not even include programs that may have been lost or concerts she gave in private homes.

But Clara was more than just an extraordinary pianist. She also had tremendous influence as a composer, teacher, and editor. In each of these roles, her work had a profound impact.

London, 1887. Clara toured England nineteen times. "She won every heart," wrote her daughter Eugenie. "When she had sat down at the piano, all the faces were lighted up from the moment when she began to play." (Elliott and Fry, Archiv des Robert-Schumann-Hauses, Zwickau)

Clara gave the first performances of all of Robert Schumann's piano music, and her sensitive interpretations helped her husband earn his place among the great composers. When Robert Schumann and Johannes Brahms were unknown, she never hesitated to include their music on her programs, and through her playing, their reputations were secured. She was also one of the first pianists in Europe to perform the work of Frédéric Chopin.

Clara's heartfelt playing brought new respect for pianists. As a young woman she was one of the few pianists to perform music from memory. Later, she honored the written notes of the score at a time when other musicians were trying to impress with flashy trills and extra notes that the composer never wrote.

In fact, Clara's work helped change the very nature of music concerts. In the early nineteenth century, concerts were like musical variety shows, with a hodgepodge of musicians sharing one performance. Audiences did not expect to spend an evening listening to one musician play just one instrument. At the very least they wanted to hear chamber music for several instruments.

When Clara was a child, a typical concert might feature Clara on piano, but then other musicians would join her on the stage. Singers were especially popular, and in the early years of her career Clara often had to include a singer on her program to keep the audience happy. Sometimes in small cities even speakers and theatrical troupes were included in concerts. The actors would recite monologues or perform scenes from famous plays.

But thanks both to Clara's marvelous musicianship and the changing tastes of audiences, by the end of her career she was able to play whole concerts of piano music. Gradually the public came to appreciate that the piano was interesting all by itself, especially when played by a musician of Clara's caliber.

Clara's work as a composer was significant, too. At her first solo con-

This original manuscript of Clara's unpublished composition "Volkslied" ("Folksong," 1840) was written on "presentation paper"—fancy paper with a colored, ornamental border—and was given to Robert as a Christmas present. Clara composed over fifty works in all.
(Archiv des Robert-Schumann-Hauses, Zwickau)

cert at age eleven, she played one of her own pieces, a practice which continued for many years. She began to compose a concerto for piano and orchestra when she was thirteen, and performed the complete work under Felix Mendelssohn's baton at sixteen. She wrote music for solo piano, chamber music, and many songs. She did not have the confidence in her composing that she had in her playing, because she saw herself more as a performing artist than a creative one. As an adult, her uncertainty about her own abilities, and her society's doubts about whether women could compose at all, limited her enthusiasm. Although both her father and her husband encouraged her to compose, she did so somewhat reluctantly. She wrote only one piece after Robert's death.

Other musicians respected Clara's creative work and would have been surprised at her mixed feelings. One colleague wrote to her in 1860: "Mendelssohn once had a big laugh because I would not believe that a woman could have composed something so solid and serious."

Several of Clara's pieces are still played frequently, especially her trio for piano, violin, and cello. All of her works have been recorded.

In addition to carrying on a phenomenal career as a performer, Clara also supported her children and grandchildren by teaching. As a piano teacher she left a legacy still resounding in the music world today. Many of her students had successful performing careers or went on to teach in the great music conservatories of Europe and America.

Clara made another important contribution: she supervised the official publication of Robert Schumann's music. In 1877, when she was

Felix Mendelssohn in 1845. Mendelssohn was the leading conductor and composer in Leipzig when Clara was a teenager. He conducted the first performance of her concerto, was a guest at her sixteenth birthday party, dedicated compositions to her, and gave her some of his original manuscripts. Clara and Robert named their son Felix after Mendelssohn.
(E. Magnus, Stadtgeschichtliches Museum, Leipzig)

The Hungarian pianist and composer Franz Liszt was Clara and Robert's friend, colleague, and rival. Clara and Franz played for each other and performed together, and Robert and Franz dedicated pieces to each other. It was Liszt who wrote about Clara in the New Music Journal *in 1854, "The lovely playmate of the Muses has become . . . a priestess." Clara did not like his renditions of Robert's music, and her friendship with Liszt cooled after Robert died.*
(A. Scheffer, Stiftung Weimarer Klassik/Museen)

nearly sixty, she undertook the monumental task of editing his collected works. With the help of Johannes Brahms and others, the last volume was finally finished in 1893. Thus, long after his death, Robert's faithful wife continued to serve the cause of his music, the same music that she had first heard as a child and that she had so long treasured.

Clara's contemporaries considered her a great musician in spite of the fact that she was a woman. From the start, her father believed she could do anything a boy could do. As a girl of twelve, she performed for Johann Wolfgang von Goethe, the greatest living German writer. Goethe presented Clara with a medal inscribed, *For the gifted artist Clara Wieck.* But the praise that most moved Frederick was Goethe's statement: "She plays with as much strength as six boys."

By the time Clara was a teenager, she was regarded as one of the greatest pianists of her time, male or female. For the rest of her life, she was seen as an equal by the male musicians and composers of her day, an extraordinary compliment. Her stellar talent, combined with the musical skills and determination learned at her father's knee, enabled her to rise above the expectations of the society in which she lived.

Clara achieved renown as a musician in a world almost completely dominated by men. In 1879, when she was teaching at the leading music conservatory in Frankfurt, the director wrote, "With the exception of Madame Schumann there is no woman and there will not be any women employed in the Conservatory. As for Madame Schumann, I count her as a man."

Brahms, 1891.
After Clara settled
in Frankfurt, Brahms
visited every year. "It
was astonishing how
full of life the house
seemed [as soon as]
Brahms set foot in
it," wrote Eugenie.
(L. Michalek, Staats-und
Universitätsbibliothek
Hamburg Carl von Ossiet-
zsky, Brahms-Archiv)

For Clara, too, music was separate from womanhood. For her, to live was to make music. "When I am able to practice regularly, then I really feel totally in my element; it is as though an entirely different mood comes over me, lighter, freer, and everything seems happier and more gratifying," she wrote in her diary in 1853. Although she was forced by circumstance to earn her living by performing, she never regarded being a musician as merely a job.

"You regard it *only* as a way to earn money," she wrote to Johannes. "I do not. I feel a calling to reproduce great works, above all . . . those of Robert, as long as I have the strength to do so. . . . The practice of art is, after all, a great part of my inner self. To me, it is the very air I breathe."

For the greater part of a century this remarkable woman thrilled audiences throughout Europe. Her dedication, combined with her serious, refined playing, inspired Robert, Johannes, and many others to describe her as a "priestess" of music. That she came in time to be revered even by critics is evident in a review in the *New Music Journal* from 1865:

> *There are many virtuosos who are not inferior to her in technique or general interpretation, but she distinguishes herself from all the rest through her high level of musicality, which gives her performances the stamp of a divine summons.*

The fiftieth anniversary of her debut at the Gewandhaus was celebrated before adoring audiences. She wrote in her diary:

The entire hall was decorated with green and gold wreaths and garlands of oak leaves. As I entered, the whole audience stood and a rain of flowers began, under which I was literally buried. . . . It was a long time before I could seat myself at the piano. Several times I felt as though I would be overwhelmed by the emotions I was feeling; I shook violently but I controlled myself and played the concerto with perfect calm and it succeeded magnificently.

The brilliant virtuoso Clara Schumann gave her last performance in 1891. As ill health and old age overtook her, she continued her teaching and editing until she was no longer physically able.

On May 20, 1896, following several strokes, Clara Schumann died at home. The last music she heard was Robert's.

At a gathering of close friends after the funeral, a soulful group of new songs by Johannes was given its first performance. Later, Brahms wrote to Clara's daughter Marie:

Deep inside us all there is something that speaks to us and drives us, almost unconsciously, and that may emerge at times as poetry or music. You will not be able to play through these songs just now because the words would be too affecting. But I beg you to regard them . . . as a true memorial to your beloved mother.

Clara Schumann, who not only inspired but also championed the greatest composers of the century, and whose playing was described by

Clara in 1878,
the year she moved
to Frankfurt to teach
at the Conservatory.
(F. v. Lenbach, Archiv
des Robert-Schumann-
Hauses, Zwickau)

critics as "elegant," "pure," "extraordinary," and "deeply artistic," went far beyond fulfilling her promise as a child prodigy.

As one reviewer put it in the *General Music Journal* in 1842, "We come to the conclusion that there is scarcely a virtuoso living today who might stand beside her in terms of virtuosity as well as in genuine artistic development."

To Clara Schumann, music was not only a gift that enabled her to bear the misfortunes of a difficult life, but a voice with which she could share her deepest experience of that life. The response she received from an adoring public is a testament to the manner in which she grasped that gift with firm and loving hands and beamed its brilliant light into the world.

Pieces of a Puzzle

HOW DO WE KNOW so much about Clara Schumann's life? Original nineteenth-century documents like letters, diaries, music manuscripts, and concert programs; articles, reviews, and advertisements from newspapers and magazines; visual materials such as photographs, drawings, and paintings and prints; and books and articles by people who knew Clara Schumann are all important sources of information for the researcher who seeks to piece together the puzzle of Clara's life. Contemporary books and articles by historians, musicologists, and other writers are also useful, while recordings of Clara's compositions, as well as those of Robert Schumann, Brahms, Chopin, Mendelssohn, and Liszt, help to complete the picture.

Clara's diary, which was started when she was seven, is one of the most important resources for information about her childhood. One of the most startling discoveries in the diary concerns Clara's relationship with her father. It turns out that Clara's diary was not entirely her own. Her father wrote all the entries for several years as if he were her, and later supervised and read everything she wrote. Sometimes the adult's handwriting and the child's appear on the same page. The very first entry, written by Frederick, reads: *My diary, begun by my father, the seventh of June, 1827, and continued by Clara Josephine Wieck.*

Even when she was a famous teenager performing for kings and queens, Clara's father continued to write in her diary as if he were her. On June 17, 1834, he wrote: *Father arrived by express coach at seven in the evening. I flew into his arms and took him right to the hotel.* And on April 8, 1833, he made this entry in Clara's diary: *My own concert at the Gewandhaus. The newspaper published a fine article about me.*

Frederick instructed Clara to copy his business letters into her diary in order to teach her to write. As a side benefit, Clara absorbed lessons in how to conduct business and manage her career, lessons which she put to good use for the rest of her life.

Clara's many letters are another primary source of information. For most of her life, Clara spent several hours every day writing letters. The published letters to and from Robert fill three volumes. If all of Clara's letters were published, they would fill several bookshelves.

Most of the primary source materials on Clara Schumann are in

The first page of Clara's diary. "My diary, begun by my father, the seventh of June, 1827, and continued by Clara Josephine Wieck." Frederick kept the diary when Clara was married and did not return it until 1859. (Archiv des Robert-Schumann-Hauses, Zwickau)

German; some are written in French or Italian. Clara's childhood diaries are currently being translated into English by Nancy B. Reich, who also translated the quotations which appear in this book. Her book, *Clara Schumann: The Artist and the Woman* (Ithaca: Cornell University Press, 1985) is an invaluable source of information, as are her numerous articles.

Eugenie Schumann's volume of reminiscences, *The Schumanns and*

At the piano.
(Music Division,
The New York
Public Library,
Astor, Lenox and
Tilden Foundations)

Johannes Brahms: The Memoirs of Eugenie Schumann (New York: The Dial Press, 1927, reprinted as *Memoirs of Eugenie Schumann* by Da Capo Press, 1985) gives a delightfully personal account of life in the Schumann family. For readers who would like to learn more about women composers, *The New Grove Dictionary of Women Composers*, edited by Julie Anne Sadie and Rhian Samuel (London: The Macmillan Press, Ltd., 1994) is an authoritative guide. Also interesting is Amy Fay's *Music Study in Germany: From the Home Correspondence of Amy Fay* (New York: Dover Publications, 1965, originally published 1880), which consists of letters sent home to America by a young piano student in nineteenth-century Germany. Those who would like to look at primary source material can see *The Complete Correspondence of Clara and Robert Schumann*, volumes 1 and 2, edited by Eva Weissweiler and translated by Hildegard Fritsch and Ronald L. Crawford (New York: Peter Lang, 1994, 1996).

EVENTS IN THE LIFE OF CLARA SCHUMANN

1816   Frederick Wieck marries Marianne Tromlitz, June 23

1819   Clara is born, September 13

1821   Clara's brother Alvin is born, August 27

1823   Clara's brother Gustav is born, January 31

1824   Marianne leaves Frederick and children, May 12

       Clara begins piano lessons, October 27

1825   Frederick and Marianne divorce, January 22

       Marianne marries Adolph Bargiel, August

1828   Frederick marries Clementine Fechner, July 3

       Clara plays at Gewandhaus, October 20

       Robert Schumann arrives in Leipzig and
          studies with Frederick

1830   Clara performs in Dresden, March 6–April 7

       Robert moves in with Clara's family

       Clara's first solo concert at Gewandhaus, November 8

1831   Clara and Frederick begin seven-month
          concert tour to Paris, late September

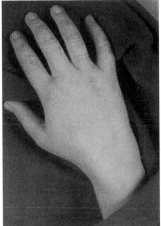

A plaster cast of Clara's broad hand. Her exceptionally long fingers, especially the little finger, enabled her to stretch across many piano keys. (Archiv des Robert Schumann-Hauses, Zwickau)

1832-34	Concert tours with Frederick in Germany
1835	Robert begins courtship of Clara
1836	Tours with Frederick continue in Germany
1837	Clara and Robert are secretly engaged, August 14
	Robert asks Frederick for Clara's hand and is rejected, September 13
	Clara and Frederick begin seven-month concert tour to Vienna, October 15
1838	Clara, 18, performs for the Austrian emperor and is named Royal and Imperial Chamber Virtuoso, March 15
1839	Clara goes to Paris without Frederick for eight months
	Clara and Robert petition court for permission to marry, June 15

This double portrait of
Robert and Clara was
carved in ivory in 1850.
(T. B. Kietz, Heinrich-Heine-
Institut, Düsseldorf)

1840	Clara stays with her mother in Berlin and
	tours with her in Germany
	Clara and Robert receive court's permission
	to marry, August 1
	Marriage of Clara and Robert, September 12
	Clara turns 21, September 13
1841	Birth of first child, Marie, September 1
1842	Concert tours accompanied by Robert
	Concert tour to Denmark without Robert
1843	Birth of Elise, April 25
1844	Four-month tour to Russia with Robert
	Schumann family moves to
	Dresden, December 13
1845	Birth of Julie, March 11
1846	Birth of Emil, February 8
	Three-month concert tour to Vienna
	with Robert, Marie, and Elise

1847   Death of sixteen-month-old Emil,
        June 11

1848   Birth of Ludwig, January 20

1849   Birth of Ferdinand, July 16

1850   Concerts with Robert in Germany

       Family moves to Düsseldorf,
        September

       Many concerts in Düsseldorf

1851   Birth of Eugenie, December 1

1852   Concerts in Leipzig, Düsseldorf,
        and other cities

1853   Johannes Brahms meets Clara and
        Robert, September 30

       Robert loses his job as director of
        orchestra

       Concert tour with Robert to Holland,
        November–December

Clara and her brother Alvin playing cards. Alvin worked as a violinist in Russia and later taught in Dresden, Germany. In 1880 they spent a summer vacation together. (R. Bendemann, Archiv des Robert-Schumann-Hauses, Zwickau)

1854	Robert attempts suicide, February 27
	Robert is hospitalized, March 4
	Birth of Felix, June 11
	Concert tours, October–December
1855–56	Concert tours
1856	Clara sees Robert in hospital for first time, July 27
	Robert dies, July 29
1857	Concert tours
	Clara moves family to Berlin, October
1869	Julie marries, September
1870	Ludwig hospitalized
1872	Clara's mother, Marianne, dies, March 10
	Julie dies, November 10
1873	Ferdinand marries, August 13
	Clara's father, Frederick, dies, October 6
1877	Elise marries, November 27
	Clara begins editing Robert's collected works

1878	Clara moves to Frankfurt, joins faculty of Conservatory
	Concerts celebrate fiftieth anniversary of Clara's debut
1879	Felix dies, February 16
1887	Ferdinand hospitalized and his six children become Clara's responsibility
1888	Sixtieth-anniversary concerts
1891	Ferdinand dies, June 6
1896	Clara suffers stroke, March 26
	Clara dies, May 20
1897	Brahms dies, April 3
1899	Ludwig dies, January 9
1928	Elise dies, July 1
1929	Marie dies, November 14
1938	Eugenie dies, September 25

This bronze bust of Clara was sculpted in 1896, the year she died. Wrote Eugenie: "Music was the true home of her soul, a materialisation [sic] of everything divine; it was her religion and her temple, the sanctuary in which it was the only god." (F. C. Hausmann, Dr. Hoch's Konservatorium, Frankfurt am Main)

INDEX

Note: Page numbers in **bold** type refer to illustrations.

art, as a gift, 41, 87, 100

Bach, Johann Sebastian, 35, 56
Baden-Baden, Clara's house in, **75**
Bargiel, Adolph (stepfather), 9, 45
Bargiel, Marianne Tromlitz Wieck
    (mother):
    Clara's residence with, 45
    first marriage of, *see* Wieck,
        Marianne Tromlitz
    Julie's residence with, 67
    remarriage of, 9
Beethoven, Ludwig van, 35, 56
Berlin, Bargiel household in, 45, 67
Bonn, Schumann children in school in,
    67
Brahms, Johannes, **80, 83, 96**
    Clara's influence in career of,
        81–82, 90
    in Eugenie's memoirs, 83, 103, 105
    on Felix Schumann, 76
    as good friend, 79–82, 95, 96, 97
    memorial to Clara from, 98
    music composed by, 79, 82, 98, 101
    Robert's thoughts on, 79, 80, 81

Brahms, Johannes *(cont.)*
    shyness of, 83

Chopin, Frédéric, 35, 90, 101
*Clara Schumann: The Artist and the
    Woman* (Reich), 103

Denmark, Clara's tour to, 53
Dresden:
    Clara's concerts in, 19–20, 22–23
    Frederick's home in, 50
    music scene in, 58
    Schumanns' move to, 57
Düsseldorf, **60**
    Clara's musical activities in, 58
    Municipal Orchestra and Chorus
      in, 58
    Robert's work in, 58–59
    Schumanns' move to, 58

Endenich, mental hospital in, **64**
England, Clara's concerts in, 62, 89

"Folksong" ("Volkslied") (C. Schumann),
    91

Franco-Prussian War, Ferdinand in, 73
Frankfurt, Clara as teacher in, 95, 96, 99

Garcia-Viardot, Pauline, **85**
General Music Journal, 30, 100
Gewandhaus, Leipzig, **11**, 15, **16, 21**
Goethe, Johann Wolfgang von, on Clara's talent, 26, 95

Joachim, Joseph, **86,** 87

Langenschwarz, Doctor, 36
Leipzig:
    Clara's concerts in, 23, 97–98
    Clara's professional debut in, 15–18, 97–98
    Gewandhaus in, **11**, 15, **16, 21**
    market square in, **3**
    music lovers in, 2, 19
    nineteenth-century life in, 2
    Schumann children in school in, 67
    Schumanns' wedding in, 4647, **47**
    Wieck home in, 2, 15
Leipzig General Music Journal, 17
List, Emilie, **81**
Liszt, Franz, **94**
    music composed by, 35, 56, 94, 101
    Schumanns' friendship with, 94

Memoirs of Eugenie Schumann (E. Schumann), 105

Mendelssohn, Felix, **93**
    as conductor, 92, 93
    Gewandhaus painted by, **16**
    music composed by, 35, 56, 93, 101
    Schumann's friendship with, 93

New Music Journal, 97
nineteenth century:
    children's rights in, 7, 31, 44
    court permission to marry required in, 44–46
    divorce in, 7
    documents from, 101
    education in, 12, 67, 69
    Leipzig in, 2
    men as dominant in, 7, 95
    musical programs in, 2, **18, 29, 36,** 90–91
    parlor games in, 2
    pregnancy hidden in, 50, 52
    servants in, 3, 57, 69
    women's rights and abilities in, 7, 92, 95

Papillons (Butterflies) (R. Schumann), 35
Paris, Clara's concerts in, 28–32
physharmonica, **31**
piano, of Clara's debut, **22**
presentation paper, **91**

Reich, Nancy B., 103

Russia, Schumanns' tour to, 54–56

St. Petersburg, Clara's concert in, 54–56
Scarlatti, Domenico, 56
Schumann, Clara Wieck, **49, 51, 55, 59, 63, 70, 89, 99**
    birth and early years of, *see* Wieck, Clara Josephine
    and Brahms's compositions, 81–82, 98
    career conflicts of, 46, 50, 71–72, 76–77, 84
    children of, 50, 57, 62, 67, 70, 72–74, 76–77, 84
    children's thoughts about, 70–72, 89
    concerts by, 66, 76, 88, 90–91, 97–98
    concert tours of, 46, 52–56, 62, 65, 73, 84, 88, 89
    correspondence of, 84, 102
    death of, 98
    debut anniversary of, 97–98
    diary of, 102–3, **103**
    as editor of Robert's work, 88, 92, 95, 98
    events in life of, 106–11
    fame of, 50, 52, 74, 95
    and father, *see* Wieck, Frederick
    Ferdinand's family supported by, 72
    flower diary of, **67**

Schumann, Clara Wieck *(cont.)*
    friends of, 79–87, **80, 81, 83, 85, 86, 93, 94, 96,** 98
    ill health of, 98
    independence of, 46, 50, 58, 65–66, 84, 92
    influence of, 81–82, 88, 90, 98
    insecurities of, 92
    money earned by, 56, 58, 65, 70, 73, 84
    and motherhood, 50, 65–77, 84
    musical expression of, 62, 64, 75, 89, 100
    musical talent of, 55–56, 95, 97, 100
    music as comfort for, 77, 87, 100
    music composed by, 57, 91–92, **91,** 101
    music in life of, 48, 50, 62, 74, 77, 84, 97
    music loved by, 84, 87, 97
    music performed from memory by, 90
    as music teacher, 57–58, 77, 88, 92, 95, 98, 99
    pianos of, **22, 31,** 48, 87
    professional demands on, 70, 73, 97
    and Robert's compositions, 82, 88, 90, 92, 95
    and Robert's death, 65–66
    and Robert's illness, 45, 61, 64, 65, 79

Schumann, Clara Wieck *(cont.)*
    royal audiences of, 54
    as single mother, 65–77
    strength of, 77, 84–85
    wedding of Robert and, 46–47
Schumann, Elise (daughter), **52, 68**
    birth of, 50
    schooling of, 67
Schumann, Emil (son):
    birth of, 57
    death of, 65, 68, 72
Schumann, Eugenie (daughter), **68, 71**
    birth of, 58
    books written by, 103, 105
    on Brahms, 83, 103, 105
    childhood of, 67, 75
    on her father's death, 71
    on her mother's career, 71, 72, 89
Schumann, Felix (son), **68, 76**
    birth of, 62
    Brahms's thoughts on, 76
    childhood of, 67
    on Clara's letter writing, 84
    illness and death of, 72, 73, 74–75, 76–77
    named after Mendelssohn, 93
Schumann, Ferdinand (son), **68, 73**
    addiction of, 72, 73
    birth of, 57
    childhood of, 67, 69
    death of, 72, 77
    family of, 72

Schumann, Ferdinand *(cont.)*
    in Franco-Prussian War, 73
Schumann, Julie (daughter), 68, **72**
    birth of, 57
    childhood of, 67
    illness and death of, 72
    marriage of, 72
Schumann, Ludwig (son), 65, **68, 74**
    birth of, 57
    childhood of, 67
    mental illness of, 73
Schumann, Marie (daughter), **51, 53, 68**
    birth of, 50
    on Brahms's playing, 79
    and devotion to Clara, 53
    schooling of, 67
Schumann, Robert, **25, 42, 49, 54, 59, 69**
    Clara's career as challenge to, 52–53, 56, 58
    Clara's friendship with, 35–36
    Clara's influence on career of, 90
    Clara's musical gift to, **91**
    Clara's talent appreciated by, 24, 40–41, 52, 92, 97
    and Clara's tours, 52–53, 54–56
    court permission to marry, 44–46
    courtship of Clara and, 44–47
    death of, 65, 66, 71
    depression of, 43, 45, 53, 56, 60–61
    Frederick as teacher of, 27, 37